REFLECTIONS

SABINA SPENCER

Illustrated by
Sean O'Neal Mason

VANTAGE PRESS
New York / Atlanta
Los Angeles / Chicago

To those whose love comforted me,
whose trust allowed me,
and whose beauty lights the world

Contents

Preface

It's hard to believe we can live as someone for many years and not know who we are. We become a person and play a role with such conviction that we don't realise we have lost our identity. We exist in a form that we have created in the hope that we will be accepted, and yet we lose ourselves in an attempt to be who we know we are not. But perhaps it is not a conscious awareness, because what we have created has overpowered us and it is easier to flow with it than to challenge it.

It's only when the individual suddenly frees itself, albeit for a moment, that we acknowledge that who we have become is not who we are and what we have is nothing but a world based on false values. Once this has happened, we may try to put the butterfly back into the chrysalis, but it cannot be done, nor will it be done, because the wings of freedom will not be folded or bent.

We have begun a process that, however hard we try to halt it, will not be stopped, nor should it be. What is occurring is the birth of the true self, not a thing that has been tailored or cast to play a part.

It's not easy to break out of a shell that has sealed itself around you, and it's painful to accept that it was you who put yourself inside it. But when you do and you can, then you have the strength to stand alone and be yourself.

The cause of this dramatic change is by no means simple to define, because we are limited by words. The key to our true self is love, not a possession of love but a sharing of ourselves. We cannot truly love until we believe in who we are; then and only then can we know what love is, what trust means, what living is for.

We no longer need material possessions to measure our wealth, we are rich in the knowledge that today is beautiful and it is ours to behold. Nothing will prevent us from seeing what we feel or restrain us from our wanderings; we are as free as the ocean and as bright as the sun, and love fills our hearts.

These words tell of the joy of discovery and the sadness of letting go; they tell of anger and despair, of life and of love.

These words belong to all those who have known the pain of shattering the shell that shielded them from reality and who have travelled through the darkest storm to find a sunny day.

Reflections

. . . and the tunnel will lead to a boundless sea of colour, where the wind will play music, the rain will kiss the flowers, the sun will feed life, and the world will be filled with the beauty and warmth of love. . . .

It's Worth the Pain

If ever you should find yourself
in darkness and alone,
you may gain comfort from these words
and strength to make it home.

It wasn't very long ago,
I passed along your way
and travelled through the darkest storm,
to find a sunny day.

It's worth the pain you're suffering
to see a world that's bright
and to be with all those who, like you,
have journeyed through the night.

The Stage

Don't drift, my friend, for simplicity's sake,
into a role where you act the fake,
saying the words that aren't yours to say,
playing the part that's not yours to play.

If you hear my words and know what that they mean,
get off the stage, leave the scene
that has turned you into someone unreal.
Stand up, my friend, be who you feel.

They Talk of Love

I hear them talk of love as if it were a game,
a joke, a toy, an object, a thing that has a name.
I hear them talk of love in terms of do's and don'ts,
of ups and downs, of ins and outs, of ifs and buts and
  won'ts.

I wonder if they know that love is living free.
It's a flower, a stream, a mountain, a bird, a rock, a tree.
It's sunshine in the winter; it's raindrops in the fall.
It's you; it's me; it's being; it is God's gift to all.

Little Tiger

O little tiger locked in a cage,
Where is your strength, your fearless rage?
Why did you get caught in that man-made snare
that lost you the freedom to breathe the fresh air?

How did you get trapped by the easy living?
Couldn't you see that all they were giving
was a false sense of values that caused you to be
locked up in a prison and not roaming free?

O little tiger, it isn't too late
to undo the chains and open the gate.
The bars are just rubber, they'll easily bend,
and we will be waiting to greet a new friend.

Who Are You?

Who are you I found to trust?
To kill a life I thought a must.
Helping me one day to find
the world I'd chosen made me blind.

Who are you who gave me sight
and lightened up my darkest night?
To give me each and every day
to live in such a special way.

Who are you who kept me warm
through fierce floods and a nightmare storm?
  You're you, you're life,
   You're friend,
  You're a love that knows
   no end. . . .

Why?

Why do we let it happen?
We give ourselves away.
Planning for tomorrow
we forget about today.

Why do we let it happen?
We lose our right to be
living, growing people,
happy being free.

Freedom of the Sea

You're grey; you're blue; you're green.
You're a nightmare; you're a dream.
You're in a state of perpetual motion.
You're oftimes called the rolling ocean.

You ebb and flow and wash the sand.
You provide a contrast to the land.
You won't be tamed; you're wild and free.
You're oftimes called the cruel sea.

Ode to a Farshit

I thought I saw a farshit
flying low across the beach;
it frolicked in the soft sea spray
beyond the tidal reach.

"A farshit?!" questioned Father.
"That's not an English bird;
in fact, I've never heard of it;
the name alone's absurd."

"But, Pa, it's such a happy bird,
it makes the world so bright,
and if you listen carefully
it'll sing to you all night!"

Discovery

They look on you with disbelief;
they really think you're strange.
They thought you too conservative
to bring about such change.

It's only then you realise
it's you who is to blame,
for taking on their standards
and joining in the game.

Now that you have done it,
you've found yourself at last;
you call it an experience
that happened in the past.

They cannot understand
the freedom that you've found,
the beauty and the colours
that in your world abound.

I Can Only Ask

I can ask you to look,
but I can't make you see.
I can ask you to listen,
but I can't make you hear.
I can ask you to touch,
but I can't make you feel.
I can show you my world,
but I can't make it yours.
We each must find our own.

To You

To you who gave me life, to whom I owe my being,
the beauty of the world, the colours I am seeing.
With you I share a love that none can take away;
it is the very sunshine that warms my every day.

To you who gave me beaches, the softness of the sand,
the forest fields and mountains, the freedom of the land.
With you I share a secret of a day so rare and pure,
a sealing of a friendship, so real, so true, so sure.

To you who gave me strength and helped me stand alone,
to wear a smile of confidence and make it on my own.
With you I share my laughter, my passion, and my heart;
though oceans flow between us, we will never part.

The Difference

How weak the created mind
that can cause us to grow blind
and make our loving stop us living,
encourage taking instead of giving.

How strong the natural mind
that can cause us to unwind
and make us happy to be caring
in a world that's filled with sharing.

Metamorphosis

It's a very interesting process
this thing called metamorphosis.
It's the breaking out of a chrysalis,
and a truly remarkable change!

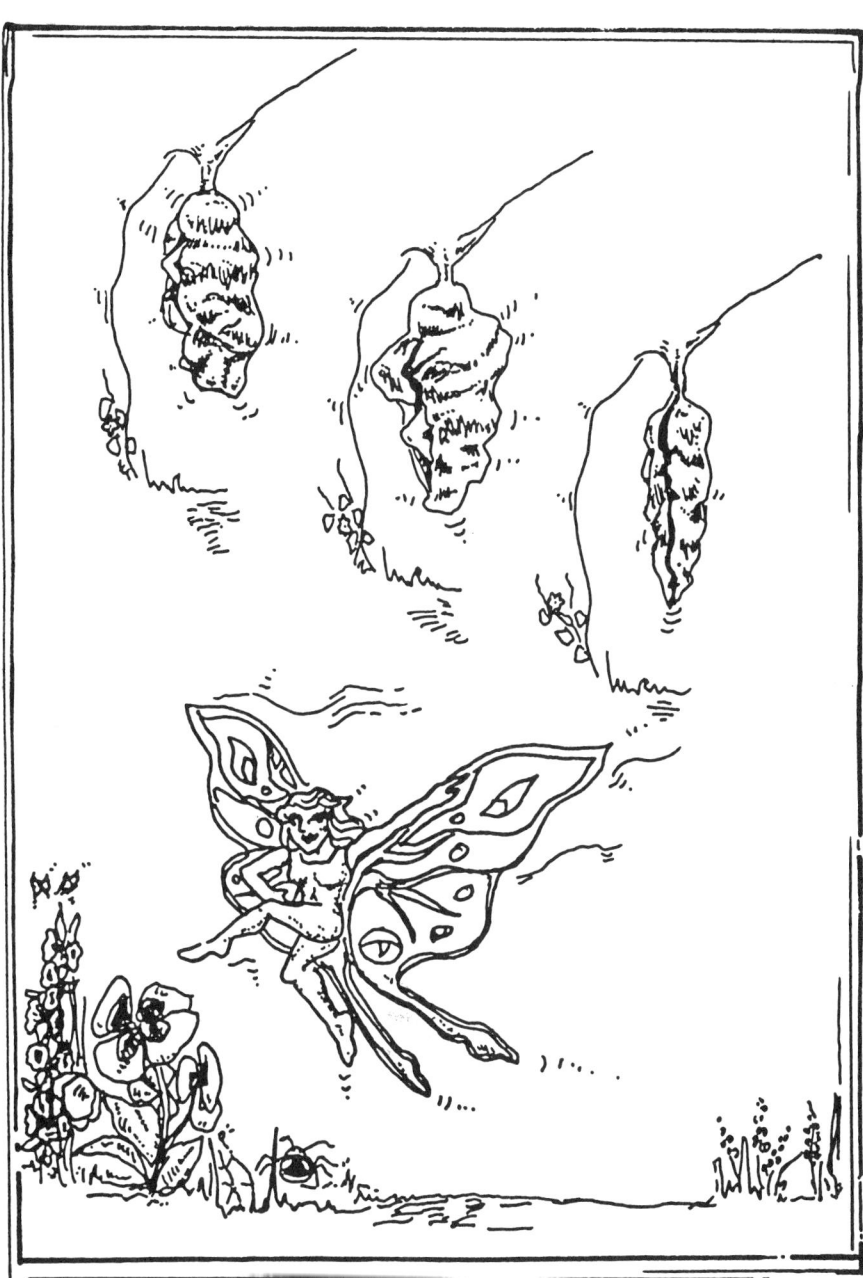

Seasons

The world spins gently round and round.
The rain drops softly to the ground.
The river flows swiftly to the sea.
A leaf falls silently from a tree.

The world spins gently round and round.
A season is lost; another is found.
Winter will come but will not stay.
The night will fade in another day.

The world spins gently round and round.
The warmth of spring will soon abound.
The sun will come to melt the snow.
The birds will sing and flowers will grow.

The world spins gently round and round.
A year will pass without a sound.
The skies of grey will turn to blue,
and summer will be when I'm with you.

Should Be

The world is full of should-be people
doing things that should be done,
selling themselves to should-be standards,
winning the things that should be won.

The world is full of should-be people
saying things that should be said,
existing in a should-be house,
sleeping in a should-be bed.

I used to be a should-be person
living life the should-be way,
but now I'm being who I am;
should-be died with yesterday!

It Just Happened

I was my parents' daughter; I became my husband's wife,
drifting to existence without ever knowing life.
It happened very easily, and I was too blind to see
that who it was that I portrayed was someone else, not me!

It's only now I realise, I lived within this lie.
I didn't choose to do it; I didn't even try.
It happened very easily and I was too blind to see
that who it was that I portrayed was someone else, not me!

I cannot make you understand the way I feel today,
to see me as I really am, to hear the words I say.
But should you ever find yourself questioning who you've
      been,
then you'll know the truth I've found and see what I have
      seen.

You Didn't Smile

You got up this morning and went to work,
      but you didn't smile.
You bought a paper and said hallo,
      but you didn't smile.
You answered the phone and wrote a letter,
      but you didn't smile.
You went to a meeting and solved a problem,
      but you didn't smile.
You caught the train home and ate your dinner,
      but you didn't smile.
You watched television and took a bath,
      but you didn't smile.
You went to bed and closed your eyes,
      but you didn't smile.
I wonder if you'll smile tomorrow.

I'm Awake

Beautiful world, where have you been?
I was told you only lived in my dream.
But now I'm awake; I'm so happy to say
you grow more beautiful every day.

Did You?

Did you see the sky today
    and smell the morning air,
or did you let the day go by
    pretending not to care?

Did you stop to question why,
    the reason for your being,
or did another day go by
    without you really seeing?

Which Someone?

If you look in a mirror, whom do you see,
Someone who's trapped or someone who's free?
Are you in darkness or are you in light?
Is it daytime or is it the night?

Is there a shadow obscuring your view,
reflecting an image that's not really you?
Or are you in sunshine, in colour, in truth,
released from the lies that lost you your youth?

Wake Up

Wake up, world.
Open your eyes.
Climb a mountain.
Reach for the skies.
Push aside those dark grey clouds.
Free yourself from the chains and the crowds!

Your Gift

Beauty was your gift to me;
I came alive through you.
Life is what you showed to me;
love is what I feel.

Pleasure is in knowing you
and always feeling strong,
unafraid to face the world,
loving you each day.

Twenty Things I Like to Do

Write a poem.
Sing a song.
Ride a horse.
Stand up strong.

Wake every morning.
Look at the sun.
Skip in the grass.
Laugh and have fun.

Run with the dawn.
Climb up a tree.
Live every day
just being me.

Help someone smile.
Hold someone's hand.
Reach for the sky.
Make love in the sand.

Walk on a beach.
Gaze at the sea.
Listen to farshits.
Stay wild and free.

To the Oak

You stand so tall, so proud, so true;
no one would ever question you.
You have a beauty all your own;
some may believe you're fully grown.
But you know different; you're not afraid
to change the colours that you made
and shed those leaves of yesterday.

Tonight

I need you close by me tonight
to know your love, to hold you tight.
To let your softness keep me warm
until the darkness turns to dawn.
I need to feel you by my side,
to kiss away the tears I've cried,
and then to lie with you as one
until the moon becomes the sun.
I need you close by me tonight
to know your love, to hold me tight.
To whisper words I long to say
until tonight becomes today.

A Friend

Once in a tender while
someone steps out of the crowd.
Someone who I can touch
and who touches me,
someone who understands.
A friend.

There is no introduction,
more of a reunion,
as if a part of me
that has been sleeping
is awakened and brought into being.

There is no separation
when our physical forms
move away from one another,
only the warm glow of knowing
that wherever I go,
my friend will be with me.

Life's Journey

I'm quieter now, more peaceful.
I've found a way of living,
not in sacrificing self;
the beauty is in giving.

It's hard to make the change,
to undergo such pain,
but once you realise who you are,
your life will be your gain.

There may be many questions
with answers hard to find,
but time will give us reason
and we'll feel peace of mind.

We're here to journey somewhere
on a road with no direction,
but we'll find courage to proceed
with love as our protection.

Nature is our comforter,
not position, state, or power.
We'll see a world of colour
in a tree, a bird, a flower.

Our friends we'll find in truth,
not in acting out a part,
but in trusting and believing
the feelings in our heart.

We're people with a purpose,
to make the world a happier place,
irrespective of our age or creed,
our colour or our race.

It's life that is our gift;
we don't see it as our right.
Our search will be in sunshine
now we've travelled through the night.

We'll sail the seas forever,
climb mountains old and new,
and when the darkness falls again,
our strength will see us through.

Gentle Death

Sweet death that takes away the pain of living,
your softness touched me gently tonight,
but I cannot follow you;
I must climb life's mountain
until the breath within me ceases.

Gentle death, you hold no darkness.
I will no longer live in fear of you,
but I cannot follow you;
I must climb life's mountain
until the breath within me ceases.

Love and Life

What is love?
Love is a feeling.
What is a feeling?
A feeling is an impulse.
What is an impulse?
An impulse is a subconscious response to a stimulus.
What is a stimulus?
Life.

Love is not measurable.
Love will not be chained.
Love asks no questions.
Love tells no lies.
Love demands nothing.
What is love?
Love is life.
Life is love.

To You

To life, to love, to Spring.
The music that you bring,
I feel, I see, I give.
We are, we touch, we live.

Inside Out

Don't hide behind your colour,
your culture, or your creed.
Hear the music in your soul,
and let your heart be freed.
Don't let the visual differences
control the way you feel.
They're only falsehoods in your mind,
and your heart is where you're real.

Throw away your prejudice.
Open your eyes and see
that who you are is a child of life
and your heart is the need to be.

Rational Man

Rational man, why fight with life
and exist in the boxes of reason?
Free yourself from the world you create
and respond to each changing season.

Rational man, why bury your soul
and wrap yourself up in confusion?
Open the door, let yourself out,
and you'll find that it's all an illusion.

Rational man, stop for a while
and look at the life you are living.
Then take the time to be who you are,
and maybe you'll think about giving.

No Words

In silence,
    you filled me with the warmth
    of a million rays of sunlight.
    You flowed through me
    like the waters of a clear mountain stream.
    You wrapped me up
    in the colours of the rainbow;
    You fed me love, life, and being.

In silence,
    I felt like a flower
    blossoming after a rain shower.
    Like a tree stretching out
    to reach the sun.
    Like a butterfly
    experiencing the beauty of flight,
    I felt alive in you.

No need for words.

A Moment

To have known you for a moment,
to feel your eyes caress me as we shared our sadness,
to feel your strength protect me as we shared our
    loneliness,
to feel your beauty fill me as we shared our joy.

To have known you for a moment,
to feel the wealth, the richness of your touch,
to feel your gentleness in me, all around me,
to feel you close and warm, entering every part of me.

To have known you for a moment,
    To feel you all my life.

Searching

. . . And as I wandered aimlessly,
I found a new direction.
A desire to cease my aloneness,
to join with you,
not to follow you,
nor to lead you,
to walk with you,
by your side
and you by mine,
to be with you
searching for life.

When

When the darkness descends,
and in my loneliness
I find my whole body
grow cold and fill with fear,
somewhere, deep inside,
a warm glow begins to flow,
and life returns to melt the icy pain.
As the greyness fades
and colours replace
the blackness that surrounded me,
my being relaxes
and I know I must trust,
trust in my feelings.
I must be who I am;
who I feel.
I must be true to myself
and allow my thoughts
to remain in harmony
with my feelings.

The Water of My Bath

If you were the water of my bath,
I would immerse my naked body in your warmth.
I would feel you flowing all around me,
filling each crevice with your liquid beauty,
if you were the water of my bath.

If you were the water of my bath,
I would soak my entire being in your softness.
I would feel you caressing all of me,
knowing your ebb and flow,
closing my eyes as you washed gently over me,
if you were the water of my bath.

And when I withdrew from you,
I would still feel you surrounding me,
for no one could touch me
so completely as you,
if you were the water of my bath.

And Yet. . . .

You're coloured black, I'm coloured white,
and yet we're both the same.
There is no need to reason why,
to fight or play a game.

You're on a different journey,
and yet mine's just like yours.
We're searching for the many keys;
we need to open doors.

You're over there, I'm over here,
and yet we're not apart.
We'll never lose the warmth we found;
we touched each other's heart.

The Birth of Love

I used to be content to play the part
that had been written for me,
until one day, without warning,
my whole being began to awaken,
and the script that had locked me in
to the existence I called life
no longer held meaning.

We didn't meet; you erupted inside me,
filling me with gentleness and strength,
with passion and excitement,
fusing my mind and body, my heart and soul.
I was witnessing my own birth,
feeling life flowing through the hollow frame
that had represented me for so many years.

I couldn't fight you; you were too powerful
to control, too beautiful to resist.
You were flooding my being.
I could feel you around me, in me.
It was a union so pure,
without sacrifice or compromise;
it was and we were.

Then you tore me into a million pieces
until my whole body ached
and my mind screamed with pain.
Part of me had to die
so you could live.
You took me from a world of justification and reason,
and I learned to trust you.

There is no distance between us,
because you know no separation, only slumber,
and as you rest, your flame becomes a flicker,
until you are rekindled with honesty,
and the freedom of life,
with no fear of dependency or restraint.
You are the birthright of every man and woman.
You're love.

I Am

All I know is that I am.
In being, I feel.
In feeling, I experience.
In experiencing, I learn.
In learning, I grow.
In growing, I live.
In living,
I am.

Your Choice

So you chose the easy path
where you won't cry but you won't laugh.
You'll always know what to do and say,
because every tomorrow will be yesterday.

So you chose the easy road
where you won't have to shed your load.
You can hide away behind your mask,
finding the answers to all that you ask.

So you chose the easy way
where life is just another day.
You can pass the time playing your games,
impressed by wealth and people's names.

So you chose to bury your soul,
portraying an image of strong self-control.
Oh, why can't you see you're allowed to reveal
the person you are in the truth that you feel?

Alone

I'm alone.
I have no age,
no colour, no religion;
I have no yesterday,
no tomorrow, no time.

I am alive.
I am today.
I am myself
and I'm alone.

I Wonder

I wonder when the sun turns cold,
will you understand?
I wonder when the sky turns black,
will you understand?
I wonder when the sea runs dry,
will you understand?
I wonder, will you ever understand?

I wonder when the mountains crumble,
will you understand?
I wonder when the trees fall down,
will you understand?
I wonder when the birds stop singing,
will you understand?
I wonder, will you ever understand?

I wonder when the earth is bloody,
will you understand?
I wonder when man ceases to be,
will you understand?
I wonder when the world is dead,
will you understand?
I wonder, will this have to happen
before you understand?

Parts of Me

Part of me is joyful;
part of me is sad.
Part of me is good;
part of me is bad.
Part of me is weak;
part of me is strong.
Part of me is right;
part of me is wrong.

Part of me is adult;
part of me is child.
Part of me is passive;
part of me is wild.
Part of me is silent;
part of me is loud.
Part of me is shy;
part of me is proud.

Part of me is growing;
part of me is sleeping.
Part of me is laughing;
part of me is weeping.
Part of me is feeling;
part of me is seeing.
All of me is searching
for those parts that are my being.

Reflections

When I think of you, I feel a sadness deep inside
like a fountain that needs to pour from within.
I want to share my sadness with you;
mine is no different from yours.
It is a reflection of our being;
it is the pain we know is ours.

When I think of you, I feel a happiness deep inside
like a flame that needs to burn from within.
I want to share my happiness with you;
mine is no different from yours.
It is a reflection of our being;
it is the joy we know is ours.

When I think of you, I feel a love deep inside
like a fountain and a flame that needs to flow and glow.
I want to share my love with you;
mine is no different from yours.
It is a reflection of our being;
it is the life we know is ours.

My Love

Please accept this gift I bring;
it's the tears that I cry and the song that I sing.
It's the heart of my life; it's the spirit in me,
and its only desire is the freedom to be.

Please accept this gift I give;
it's all that I am and the reason I live.
It's the thread of my being; it's the feelings in me
and its only desire is the freedom to be.

Please accept this gift I send;
it's the joy of peace in the trust of a friend.
It's the breath of my body; it's the love deep in me
and its only desire is the freedom to be.

Our World

The earth is the garden in which we will roam;
the trees and the flowers will colour our home.
The songs of the birds will fill us with cheer;
they'll keep our hearts warm and shield us from fear.

The sea is the stage on which we will play;
the winds and the waves will be friends in the day.
The moon and the stars will shine in the night;
they'll protect us from darkness and feed us with light.

The world is the space in which we will live;
the love that we feel is the gift we will give.
The spirits within us will allow us to be;
they'll grant us the beauty of the earth and the sea.

I, Like This Earth

I have known the loneliness of a desert,
the solitude of a mountain,
the denseness of a jungle.

I have experienced the power of a river,
the anger of a volcano,
the lushness of a forest.

I have felt the coldness of an icy wind,
the gentleness of a shower of rain,
the warmth of the summer sun.

And now, I, like this earth, am
all these things, and they are all of me.

—They allow my being.

The Children

Let them laugh; let them weep.
Let them play; let them sleep.
Let them feel; let them see.
Let them live; let them be.
Let them learn; let them grow.
Let them out; let them go.
—Allow them their freedom.

There Comes a Time

Though you may search and try to find
a reason for all that you see,
there comes a time to accept just what is
and allow it to breathe and to be.

Though you may listen and try to relate
to an experience of a similar kind,
there comes a time to let go of the past
and to live with an open mind.

Though you may stop and try to explain
all that you do and you say,
there comes a time to trust in yourself
and to grow in the world of today.

Though you may question and try to equate
the feelings that flow through your being,
there comes a time to open your eyes
and grant your heart the power of your seeing.